ABOUT THE AUTHOR

Avery Crozier's EAT THE RUNT was honored in the
2001 Top 10 Off Broadway Plays listing by the *New York
Daily News*. In 1996 Avery was one of the writers for
Endangered Species, a monologue play presented at
the Interact Theater in North Hollywood as part of its
Interactivity festival. In PISHTACO and WALKING TO
BUCHENWALD, Avery's second and third full-length
plays, Avery once again exploits the temporal nature of
theater with non-gender-specific roles that can be cast
male or female.

CHARACTERS & SETTING

MERRITT, *an interviewee*
CHRIS, *a grantwriter*
JEAN, *a human resources coordinator*
ROYCE, *a director of development*
HOLLIS, *a curator of modern art*
SIDNEY, *a trustee*
PINKY, *a museum director*
NEW MERRITT, *an interviewee*

In the original production, eight actors of a variety of ethnicities and genders each memorized all eight roles, and the audience cast the play each night. As this proved to be an effective way to explore the play's themes (with more than 40,000 possible variations), this version of the script incorporates the audience participation element.

Doubling (if desired to reduce the cast to five) may be as follows: ROYCE/SIDNEY *and* PINKY/JEAN/HOLLIS.

The action takes place in various places throughout an art museum. The time is the present.

Some roller chairs, a small cafe table, and a desk, with perhaps some framed exhibition posters on the walls.
A couple of entrances.

Costume note: All characters wear business attire.

Originally produced in New York by Mefiso Theater Company.

EAT THE RUNT

Avery Crozier

BROADWAY PLAY PUBLISHING INC
56 E 81st St., NY NY 10028-0202
212 772-8334 fax: 212 772-8358
BroadwayPlayPubl.com

EAT THE RUNT
© Copyright 2007 by Avery Crozier

First printing: June 2007
I S B N: 0-88145-341-2

Book design: Marie Donovan
Word processing: Microsoft Word
Typographic controls: Ventura Publisher
Typeface: Palatino
Printed and bound in the U S A

ACT ONE

(CHRIS *walks in with* MERRITT. *Both wear business attire.*
MERRITT *looks nervous.*)

CHRIS: Now, I don't wanna scare you, but we usually
call Human Resources the Anti-Personnel Department.
And Jean is kinda the ultimate in rigid bureaucracy—
didn't even want me to come get you at staff entrance
cause you might—I dunno—sue us for harassment or
something if I shook your hand too long. Official
policy—in all the years I've never seen anyone in
Human Resources smile. So don't be nervous. It's going
to be a long day.

(JEAN *appears, unsmiling.*)

CHRIS: Jean, this is Merritt, the Grants Manager
candidate.

JEAN: *(Icily)* Welcome.

CHRIS: I'll be back in a little bit to take Merritt to see
Royce. Good luck. *(Disappears)*

JEAN: Have a seat.

(MERRITT *starts to sit in a chair.*)

JEAN: Nnnn! *(Points.* MERRITT *sits in the other chair.* JEAN
hands MERRITT *some forms.)* I don't need these done right
away—just drop them off by lunchtime. *(Sits and refers
to a resume)* All the way from California. Fundraising
must be so easy there, with all that entertainment
industry money floating around. You'll find it's nothing

like Los Angeles here. The climate is a real deterrent for people from warmer places, so I hope you're serious about your candidacy. The Development Department is obviously quite serious about you, flying you here, putting you up in luxury accommodations. In my opinion it's usually a waste of time—the museum's better off promoting from within. Good for morale. Cheaper, too. *(Sighs)* But here we are. How are you?

MERRITT: My anus hurts. It's not hemorrhoids exactly, although I've had them before. When I was only thirteen I had one that thrombosed and the doctor had to lance it on an outpatient basis and there was so much blood the nurse had to leave the room cause she was gonna be sick. But like I said, it isn't hemorrhoids this time, probably some kinda non-specific rectalitis, some kinda infection, cause I can feel the lymph node right here— *(Rubs groin)* —swelling up like it does when my anus gets infected, which it does every now and then. I've just got a bad luck butt. This time I think it's from sitting all day on the plane after rather hyperbolic anal sex last night. Don't worry, I was safe and everything. Used a dildo. Can't be too careful these days. But it was one of those oversized ones so it loosened me up something awful. God, I hope I don't break wind during one of these interviews. That would be pretty embarrassing.

JEAN: *(After staring for a long moment)* I...I...have hemorrhoids, too. You poor thing! I know exactly how you feel.

(They reach out to each other and scoot their roller chairs across the room to embrace. JEAN *pats* MERRITT *comfortingly. After a moment* CHRIS *appears.)*

CHRIS: Tears, already?

JEAN: *(Smiling broadly as they both stand)* Not at all. I think Merritt will fit right in here at the museum.

CHRIS: Thanks, Jean.

(JEAN *disappears as* CHRIS *leads* MERRITT *away.*)

CHRIS: Looks like you made a good first impression. Jean usually hates everyone on sight. Job interviews are a lot like fundraising itself. Really just stage management—making sure the right people say the right things to the other right people at the right time.

MERRITT: I think I've got my lines down.

CHRIS: Good. Can I get you anything? Coffee or how about a danish?

MERRITT: Nice of you, but no thanks.

CHRIS: Just want you to be as comfortable as possible.

MERRITT: I really appreciate it. But I'm fine. I'm good at this stuff.

CHRIS: Your next appointment is Royce, who'd be your boss— *(Smiles)* —If you get the job. My boss, too, for now. *(Points to self)* Grants Coordinator, working for you— *(Points to* MERRITT*)* —Grants Manager, working for Royce—

(ROYCE *appears, carrying a bucket.*)

CHRIS: —Director of Development.

ROYCE: *(Shaking* MERRITT*'s hand)* Thanks, Chris. Come back after we're done to take Merritt to Curatorial.

CHRIS: All right, but I'm in the middle of those trustee letters for your signature.

ROYCE: Which?

CHRIS: Trustee annual giving.

ROYCE: That's not your job.

CHRIS: Last Thursday you asked me—

ROYCE: Oh, yes. Aren't they almost done? We're late as it is.

CHRIS: This afternoon at three.

ROYCE: I need them by lunch. And make yourself generally available to take Merritt around. *(Touching* MERRITT*)* Wouldn't want you getting lost and becoming part of the collection. *(To* CHRIS*)* See you in a few.

*(*CHRIS *just stares a moment, then leaves.* ROYCE *gestures toward a chair.)*

ROYCE: Please.

*(*MERRITT *sits.)*

ROYCE: Sometimes the staff needs a little encouragement. I hope you're up to that. *(Pulls out a resume)* In an absolute fit of optimism I already called your references. Everyone in L A speaks very highly of you, especially Randy Kanschat.

MERRITT: I try not to choose hostile references.

ROYCE: Randy's not your current boss.

MERRITT: Randy has been elevated to V P of External Affairs, but we're still friends.

ROYCE: External Affairs?

MERRITT: Any public contact with the museum.

ROYCE: I take it your current boss doesn't know you're interviewing.

MERRITT: I hope not.

ROYCE: We'll keep it *entre nous.*

MERRITT: Thank you.

ROYCE: Why would anyone want to leave Southern California? Beaches, sunshine, Disneyland.

MERRITT: Earthquakes, wildfires...Disneyland.

ROYCE: Don't you have attachments?

MERRITT: Attachments?

ROYCE: It's illegal to ask you this directly, but I notice no— (*Touches ring finger*)

MERRITT: Oh. No, I'm not married.

ROYCE: But...involved?

MERRITT: I live with someone.

(ROYCE *just smiles.*)

MERRITT: Cory.

(ROYCE *smiles.*)

MERRITT: Who doesn't know I'm here, incidentally.

ROYCE: Really?

MERRITT: Cory's had some success in L A finally— acting. A bit of ninety-nine-seat theater, two commercials this year, and a movie of the week starring Mary Tyler Moore.

ROYCE: Oh, good for her.

MERRITT: Her?

ROYCE: Mary. Haven't seen her in anything for a while.

MERRITT: *Flirting With Disaster.*

ROYCE: Oh. Pardon me.

MERRITT: The movie.

ROYCE: Oh. Yes. But that was years ago.

MERRITT: So it's a big deal. The MOW.

ROYCE: I can imagine.

MERRITT: I hadda sorta sneak out of town. Fictional funeral of a friend Cory doesn't know.

ROYCE: Oh, bad karma. What if the friend actually dies? What will you tell Cory when you have to go to the real funeral?

MERRITT: By then Cory may not care where I am.

ROYCE: Oh, so pessimistic. Or is that optimistic? Your resume is impressive. And as I said I've checked you out. But what do you consider your most recent success? What's given you the most gratification?

MERRITT: Besides being invited to this interview?

ROYCE: Oh, I'm easy. We're going to put you through the wringer today. Don't be too flattered just yet.

MERRITT: Wring me. I've been looking forward to it.

ROYCE: Interviews don't make you nervous? They make me tense, no matter which side of the table I'm on. *(Touches instep)* I get a knot right here.

MERRITT: Is it there now?

ROYCE: Yes, and it's awful. Right at that place you can't get enough leverage to massage.

MERRITT: I can.

ROYCE: Only if you're an orangutan.

MERRITT: Yours. I can get enough leverage for yours. May I?

ROYCE: *(Kicking off a shoe)* Well...as long as we don't tell Inhuman Resources.

MERRITT: *(Starts massaging ROYCE's foot)* You're very tight.

ROYCE: It's been said. Oooh.

MERRITT: Does that hurt?

ROYCE: Deliciously. *(Moving foot to MERRITT's crotch)* Harder.

MERRITT: *(Rubbing with foot in crotch)* You sure?

ROYCE: If I thought we could get away with it,
I'd lie down on the floor right now.

MERRITT: Oh?

ROYCE: So you could walk on my back. You look
like the perfect weight.

MERRITT: It's been said.

(They grunt, moan and murmur as they chat, ROYCE'*s foot
pushing hard into* MERRITT'*s groin.)*

ROYCE: I hope you won't find our interview process too
formal.

MERRITT: I'll survive. Interviews are inherently artificial.

ROYCE: Putting your best foot forward.

MERRITT: Yet you never know if you're getting to know
the real person.

ROYCE: Only pieces.

MERRITT: Trying to make them cohere.

ROYCE: Trying to tear down a facade.

MERRITT: Searching for contradictions.

ROYCE: Patterns.

MERRITT: Exaggerations.

ROYCE: Truth.

MERRITT: It's all just personalities.

ROYCE: Compatibility.

MERRITT: Liking someone or not.

ROYCE: You're rough.

MERRITT: Sorry.

ROYCE: It's good rough. Almost a religious experience. *(Licks front teeth as in the old Pearl Drops commercial)*

MERRITT: How much more time do we have?

ROYCE: *(Looking at watch)* Fuck. You have to run over to Hollis.

MERRITT: The curator?

ROYCE: Yes, and you can't be late. You're on a strict schedule today so you can see everybody before lunch. *(Standing)* That was exquisite. I'm resurrected.

MERRITT: Deep tissue. Deeper later?

ROYCE: *(Grabbing* MERRITT *for support while putting on shoe.)* After you're hired. We do have to be careful. This is a wonderful museum and people here work very hard, but not everyone is a soft touch like me. You never know who might be out to get you.

MERRITT: Should I guess who? Is that part of the evaluation?

ROYCE: Our Grants Coordinator, for instance.

MERRITT: Really? Chris seems so nice, so helpful. Full of advice.

ROYCE: Chris was a candidate for your job. This job. Your almost job.

MERRITT: But is no longer a candidate?

ROYCE: Not a serious one. Not to me anyway. But I have a feeling Chris still harbors hopes. So take any advice with a grain of salt. A cube of salt. A salt lick. Sorry, I'm from the farm. You know what a salt lick is?

MERRITT: For the cows?

ROYCE: Oh, you know! I used to lick it sometimes when I was little.

MERRITT: Me, too. At my grandparents' farm.

ROYCE: So now we have a secret.

CHRIS: *(Appearing)* Already?

ROYCE: Pardon?

CHRIS: Are you ready?

ROYCE: Yes, where've you been?

CHRIS: Proofing the trustee letters—

ROYCE: Hollis is waiting, and you know how that can be.

CHRIS: *(To* MERRITT*)* Shall we jog?

ROYCE: Thanks, Merritt. I'll re-connect with you after lunch. *(Disappears)*

CHRIS: So. How'd it go with Royce?

MERRITT: Very well, I think.

CHRIS: *(Surprised)* Really?

MERRITT: We seemed to bond.

CHRIS: No kidding. Royce is a tough—nut—to crack.

MERRITT: Guess I just had the right cracker. Royce even warned me not to trust you.

(They both laugh. MERRITT *stops laughing first.)*

MERRITT: Um...who's next? The scary curator?

CHRIS: Hollis isn't so bad. Just a little hostile to the Development Office. Never quite enough money for contemporary acquisitions. If you live through it, Hollis can take you to Sidney, our trustee. *(Points)* Right through there.

*(*CHRIS *leaves.* MERRITT *heads in the direction* CHRIS *indicated and almost runs into* HOLLIS, *who is dressed in the latest fashion, wears sunglasses, and carries a mug of coffee.)*

HOLLIS: You look lost—you must be the Grants candidate.

MERRITT: *(Shaking hands)* That's right. Merritt. Are you Hollis?

HOLLIS: *(With a lot of energy, almost jittery)* Pretty damn inconsiderate of them to make you find your appointments on your own.

MERRITT: I've been doing all right.

HOLLIS: *(Offering a business card)* Do you have a card?

MERRITT: *(Searching)* Sure.

HOLLIS: *(Gestures to a seat)* Want anything? They been pumping you full of coffee?

MERRITT: No, actually.

HOLLIS: And this is my last drop. I'm trying to ration. Sorry. Puts me right over the top.

MERRITT: I can't seem to find my wallet. I'll send you a card.

HOLLIS: Great. Well, let me tell you my problem. I don't understand why you're being interviewed.

MERRITT: I'm sorry?

MERRITT: You don't really want the job, do you?

MERRITT: I flew all the way from California.

HOLLIS: Sure you didn't just come out of obligation to Randy Kanschat?

MERRITT: You know Randy?

HOLLIS: No, but I know...things. Randy set this up, and you don't want to disappoint your mentor by declining the invitation.

MERRITT: Randy's just my reference.

HOLLIS: You can't move here. What about Cory?

MERRITT: You do your research.

HOLLIS: I don't like walking into an interview blind.

MERRITT: Your information is incomplete. I am intensely interested in this job. This is a great museum. Who wouldn't want to work here?

HOLLIS: *(Laughs) Your* information is incomplete. Think you're more qualified than Chris?

MERRITT: I don't know Chris' qualifications. Been here a long time, I know that.

HOLLIS: A hell of a long time. Damn good fundraiser. Got me lots of exhibition grants over the years.

MERRITT: That's my reputation as well.

HOLLIS: Everyone in the museum except Royce thinks Chris should get the job. Which is, of course, why Royce will hire someone else.

MERRITT: I take it you're not a fan.

HOLLIS: In Royce's view, fundraising is the world's oldest profession.

MERRITT: Ah.

HOLLIS: Never wears underwear.

MERRITT: I hadn't noticed.

HOLLIS: It's *very* apparent.

MERRITT: Um...back to my candidacy—

HOLLIS: Oh, had we strayed?

MERRITT: It is Royce's decision.

HOLLIS: Unfortunately. But Royce is clever. This round robin interview gets buy-in from the rest of the staff. If you can charm us.

MERRITT: Gosh, I like your hair.

HOLLIS: *(Laughs)* Enough of this bullshit. What do you know about the curatorial side of an art museum?

MERRITT: As much as a grantwriter needs to.

HOLLIS: Do you feel you can work within our structure?

MERRITT: I open structures.

HOLLIS: Aggressive. Nice. Saying what I want to hear. Think you've figured me out, my style?

MERRITT: I saw your *Ghosts of Modernism* show.

HOLLIS: Uh-huh?

MERRITT: Good thesis. Some nice selections.

HOLLIS: Some? *Newsweek* called it authoritative.

MERRITT: Too authoritative for my taste. The text panels were so definitive. And the poor, deceived public thinks any opinion put forth by an art museum is absolute fact, cultural gospel.

HOLLIS: This is the fault of my didactic panels?

MERRITT: Your opinion was disguised as fact. If you'd been a bit more speculative in the wall panels, people would have felt their own arguments were invited, if not actually valued.

HOLLIS: You're suggesting we encourage the public to *think* about art?

MERRITT: It's a more engaging approach.

HOLLIS: Engaging? Sounds like battle.

MERRITT: You enjoy battle.

HOLLIS: You're quick but completely full of shit.

MERRITT: Thank you. That's my job.

HOLLIS: To lie?

MERRITT: If I'm to make you look good. All grant applications are, by nature, lies. They outline hopes—which are lies. Plans, dreams, not reality. By no means reality. You're selling the funder a bill of goods, padding the budget to include overhead and hidden administrative costs.

HOLLIS: Your entire profession is therefore unethical.

MERRITT: I support your profession with my lies.

HOLLIS: But how good are you?

MERRITT: Since we sat down I've told you several lies, twice as many half-truths, and embellished most of the rest. Or not—maybe this is the lie. Can you sort it out?

(HOLLIS *shrugs.*)

MERRITT: Grantwriting.

HOLLIS: *(Standing)* I think I know what I need to know. I'll take you to Sidney.

MERRITT: *(Standing)* A fair assessment-that proves my point. You think you know what you need to know. Enough to create your own narrative.

HOLLIS: *(As they start walking)* I can see why you're looking for a job.

MERRITT: Pure speculation. Just like everyone else, you're addicted to narrative. It's the curse of modern society.

HOLLIS: People have craved stories since before *Gilgamesh.*

MERRITT: These days our narratives are too fractured. M T V, the internet. It's a struggle to figure out what's going on.

HOLLIS: We've adapted.

MERRITT: We just think we have. It puts us on edge, this sense of incompleteness, not knowing the end. We get insomnia, indigestion—some commit murder to compensate.

HOLLIS: Crap!

MERRITT: Most serial killers create narratives they can control. And they know their story will end not just with the deaths of their victims, but with their own capture, judgment and execution. A story with an ending, if not a happy one.

HOLLIS: *(Shaking hands)* Well, here's our happy ending—we must part. Sidney's right through there.

MERRITT: I take it you don't buy my theory.

HOLLIS: I don't buy shit.

MERRITT: Funny, I heard different from our curator of modern art.

HOLLIS: Valerie? If you take her seriously—

MERRITT: Not long after you were hired, hipster that you are, you developed a cocaine addiction that outstripped even your outrageous salary—

HOLLIS: What a bitch!

MERRITT: In order to pay for it you started taking kickbacks from dealers on some pretty crappy paintings you purchased for the museum—a lot of Kostabis if I'm not mistaken—

HOLLIS: You are mistaken—

MERRITT: But your debts kept piling up and you resorted to actually smuggling small art objects into the country from Europe and Japan—got caught once—

HOLLIS: What the fuck is she telling people? Who does she say this to?

MERRITT: Everybody. *(Peering)* Is that Sidney? But that's nothing compared to what you finally did—

HOLLIS: What?

SIDNEY: *(Appearing)* Are you Merritt? I'm Sidney. I'm on the development committee of the board.

MERRITT: *(Shaking hands)* Pleasure.

HOLLIS: What did I do?!

MERRITT: I don't think you want me to— *(Gestures toward SIDNEY)* —I need to talk to Sidney, and not about *that—*

HOLLIS: Here's my card.

MERRITT: *(Refusing the card)* You already gave me one.

HOLLIS: Call me or drop by as soon as—

MERRITT: Every minute is booked—

HOLLIS: When you get back to L A, then. From the airport, the plane!

MERRITT: I'll try.

(HOLLIS disappears.)

SIDNEY: You seem to have made quite an impression on Hollis.

MERRITT: *(Suddenly with a rather nasal southern accent that continues throughout the scene)* You know how folks get when they want to hear the ending of a good story.

SIDNEY: I've been hearing good stories about you.

MERRITT: Not a word of truth, I guarantee.

SIDNEY: *(Gesturing to a chair)* Something to drink? Soft drinks are all we have, I'm afraid. Which is no problem for me, because I don't drink. Alcohol.

MERRITT: Pity. A good rum-n-Coke would get me through these interviews right slick. Kidding.

SIDNEY: Good, good. *(Takes two Cokes and hands one to MERRITT.)* Plain Coke all right?

MERRITT: Thank you kindly.

SIDNEY: Where are you from? I didn't notice your accent at first.

MERRITT: Oklahoma. My people have been there since the Trail of Tears.

SIDNEY: You're Native American?

MERRITT: Part, anyway.

SIDNEY: What...tribe...er...nation?

MERRITT: Not sure. Probably more than one. Almost everybody black in Oklahoma has some Indian blood.

SIDNEY: Black?

MERRITT: African American.

SIDNEY: You're...African American?

MERRITT: Of course.

SIDNEY: Pardon me, but your features aren't particularly...African.

MERRITT: You want me to sing *Old Man River*?

SIDNEY: No, no, I'm sorry—it's just—never mind. Oklahoma. What's it like there?

MERRITT: Racist.

SIDNEY: I would imagine. The education system—

MERRITT: That's why I moved to California, because of prejudice.

SIDNEY: But—pardon me again—you can't have suffered too much from—discrimination—

MERRITT: Why not?

SIDNEY: Surely—even in Oklahoma—you can—for lack of a better word—pass. People wouldn't see you as—

MERRITT: Black?

SIDNEY: Well, yes.

MERRITT: I'm sure you mean that as a compliment—

SIDNEY: No, no! I'm not placing a value on—

MERRITT: Most people find racial issues very awkward. I live them every day.

SIDNEY: I'm sorry if I'm behaving awkwardly. I've dealt with prejudice in my life too, as you can imagine, so—

MERRITT: Really?

SIDNEY: Well, of course, even today some people—

MERRITT: Do you personally know any black people? Invite them over for drinks, dinner?

SIDNEY: I don't drink—but dinner, certainly!

MERRITT: Of course you do. Even when you don't know it.

SIDNEY: I suppose that's possible....

MERRITT: People of African descent are everywhere, even when you can't see us.

SIDNEY: Apparently.

MERRITT: You know about the five black U S presidents?

SIDNEY: Oh—now, come on—

MERRITT: Unimaginable, is it?

SIDNEY: Well, certainly...unlikely.

MERRITT: You seem to be operating with some fairly rigid definitions.

SIDNEY: I see, you don't mean *black* black. You mean some of them may have had a bit of African ancestry?

MERRITT: What kind of distinction are you trying to make? What is *black* black?

SIDNEY: We seem to be getting in a bit of a tangle here. I'm sure Royce intended for us to talk about your grant-writing abilities.

MERRITT: You don't believe me, do you?

SIDNEY: About what, exactly? I suppose a person can be—

MERRITT: Jefferson, Jackson, Lincoln, Harding and Eisenhower.

SIDNEY: *(After a moment)* Eisenhower?

MERRITT: His wife *was* named Mamie.

SIDNEY: But he didn't seem—

(MERRITT *just stares.*)

SIDNEY: I mean, there was nothing to suggest—

(MERRITT *stares.*)

SIDNEY: He was German, wasn't he, or Dutch? By descent—

MERRITT: We're all descended from Eve, genetically speaking, that prehistoric woman in Africa—

SIDNEY: Then you could as easily say *everyone's* black!

MERRITT: Is that somehow offensive to you?

CHRIS: *(Appearing)* Sounds like you're having too much fun.

SIDNEY: Oh, Chris, so good to see you.

MERRITT: Am I talking to the Director next?

CHRIS: Pinky only has a few minutes, so we need to get over there.

SIDNEY: And I'm overdue for a committee meeting. Terrific to meet you, Merritt.

(SIDNEY *holds out a hand.* MERRITT *responds with a soul handshake.*)

MERRITT: Thank you. This has been most enlightening.

SIDNEY: Indeed. Good-bye. (*Rushes off*)

CHRIS: (*As they walk*) How was that?

MERRITT: (*Dropping the accent*) Let me ask you this. I assume you like working here.

CHRIS: Of course.

MERRITT: Why?

CHRIS: The collection is incredible.

MERRITT: The art or the people?

CHRIS: Both. The people are great.

MERRITT: Some real characters.

CHRIS: Exactly. While the art is so...solid. So beautiful and perfect.

MERRITT: It's about contrast? Human frailty versus artistic purity?

CHRIS: Sort of. But art grows out of human imperfection. Artists aren't perfect either.

MERRITT: I keep expecting one of these bozos to poke an elbow through a painting.

CHRIS: They seem to like you.

MERRITT: Really? You've been getting feedback?

CHRIS: Some. Royce is hearing more, of course.

MERRITT: So I'm doing all right?

CHRIS: The Director's opinion is the make-or-break. Isn't sposed to be, but it is. No pressure.

PINKY: *(Appears.)* Good morning. You must be Merritt.

CHRIS: I've got to pick someone else up at staff entrance, but I'll be back in ten or fifteen to take you to lunch.

MERRITT: Thanks, Chris.

*(*CHRIS *disappears.)*

MERRITT: Very nice to meet you finally. You have a wonderful museum, with terrific people working for you.

PINKY: That's good to hear. Please make yourself at home.

MERRITT: Thank— *(Starts to sit, stops suddenly, gasps quietly.)* Do you drive a dark green Mercedes?

PINKY: Yes, why?

MERRITT: Oh...never mind. *(Sits down)*

PINKY: Did you see it in staff parking? Is it all right?

MERRITT: No.

PINKY: What?

MERRITT: No, I didn't see it. It's all right.

PINKY: Good.

MERRITT: For now.

PINKY: Do you know something I don't about my car?

MERRITT: Not— *(Thinking hard)* —Exactly. Just be very careful driving home. *(Smiles)* Well. I'm so impressed with the changes you've made at the museum in the last fifteen years. I came here once or twice when I was little and found it scary.

PINKY: We've tried to make it more user-friendly, if I may indulge in jargon. Did you grow up around here?

MERRITT: No, I'm from New Orleans originally.

PINKY: You've done away with any accent.

MERRITT: Had to. A Southern accent makes a person sound, well, not very bright. No one's going to just hand you a job, a decent job, and if you sound like your own mother's cousin—

PINKY: I understand. We've all worked hard to get where we are.

MERRITT: But so many people think they shouldn't have to, have you noticed?

PINKY: How do you mean?

MERRITT: Affirmative action, most obviously. Why should people get special rights, a leg up, just cause they check off a certain box on a census form? You're not seriously considering the job at the Met?

PINKY: Excuse me, you sort of switched tracks on me there. The Metropolitan Museum of Art?

MERRITT: You don't want to go to New York.

PINKY: I don't know what you're talking about.

MERRITT: Perhaps I'm mistaken. I got kind of—for lack of a better word I'll call it an impression—that you were short-listed for the directorship of the Met.

PINKY: I...really can't talk about that.

MERRITT: I understand. Sorry that just popped out. I was born with a caul and I see things sometimes.

PINKY: A call? Like to the ministry?

MERRITT: No, C-A-U-L, born with a veil, afterbirth actually, stuck to my face. In New Orleans they say that means you have special...abilities. Never mind. I'll try to block it out.

PINKY: You were saying? Affirmative action? I'm interested because it's something we're grappling with, especially on the board level.

MERRITT: It's ridiculous. The opposite of survival of the fittest. If the best person doesn't get the job, where are we all—as a species—headed?

PINKY: If you're the best person, I'm sure you'll get the job.

MERRITT: Oh, I'm not talking about myself. It's a pervasive problem, bigger than affirmative action, really. I don't wanna sound cold-hearted, but we as a society spend too much time guarding the rights of the unfit. And I'm not saying they should have any fewer rights than anyone else, but they certainly shouldn't have *more*.

PINKY: Were they showing *The Fountainhead* on the plane?

MERRITT: No. But see, there's an example. You'll judge me partly on my understanding of your joke, the cultural recognition of Ayn Rand's philosophy in the novel and the movie. My education and ability give me an advantage rather than some unrelated factor like ethnicity.

PINKY: Sounds like you think Ayn Rand doesn't go far enough.

MERRITT: Think of all the regulations we have in this country to protect stupid people. To ensure that they survive, reproduce, and contribute—disastrously— to the gene pool. The closest we've come to this kind of genetic crisis is the nineteenth century's preservation of hemophilia in the royal families of Europe.

PINKY: Are you suggesting—perhaps this is a suitable metaphor—that we let the hemophiliacs bleed to death?

MERRITT: Exactly. Why put big warning labels on cigarettes and let so-called victims sue tobacco companies? If they're dumb enough to start smoking, let them die. We don't need their dopey, suicidal genes. Better yet, increase the nicotine and carcinogens in cigarettes to hook them quicker and kill them before they have a chance to reproduce.

PINKY: Certainly an iconoclastic view.

MERRITT: It's just practical for the species. When my dog had puppies, she ate the runt. Why can't we have that much sense?

PINKY: A modest proposal.

MERRITT: *(Laughs)* See? See?! I'm enjoying this, aren't you? We've both read Jonathan Swift, we've both read Ayn Rand, we've both gotten more than a little physical with Royce— *(Gasps. Silence)* Shit. I'm sorry. That caul again. I just saw you and Royce—you know—and the image shot from my brain to my mouth before I had time to stop it. *(Silence)* Forget I said a thing. I should go—I'm sure you're intensely occupied with the affairs of the museum—I mean the *business* of the museum.

PINKY: Yes.

MERRITT: Sorry I blathered on and on about natural selection, but it is pretty important to me and, in fact, the whole human race, if anybody would pay attention. Think of the money we'd save and the advancement of humanity if we did away with drug rehabilitation and just let weak people O D, shut down suicide hotlines— *(Gasps)*

PINKY: My brother committed suicide when he was seventeen.

MERRITT: I know. I'm sorry.

PINKY: You'd better go.

ROYCE: *(Bursting into the room)* Pinky, we have a problem.

PINKY: I'd say so.

ROYCE: Hello, Merritt. I'm still not quite sure what's going on, but something very strange has happened, is happening, and I tried to keep it out of your hair but the timing's off and—

NEW MERRITT: *(Off)* All I need to do is confront—

CHRIS: *(Bursting in)* Royce, I tried to stop—

NEW MERRITT: *(Following CHRIS)* I'm really sorry to do this— *(Sees MERRITT)* —But I was right.

PINKY: Royce, who is this?

NEW MERRITT: I'm Merritt. The candidate for the Grants Manager position.

MERRITT: No, you're not!

PINKY: *(Gesturing toward MERRITT)* Then who is this?

MERRITT: I'm Merritt!

NEW MERRITT: That's Cory.

MERRITT: No!

ROYCE: Cory you live with in Los Angeles? Who acts?

NEW MERRITT: Yes. *(To MERRITT)* I can't believe you.

MERRITT: What are you doing? Royce, this is crazy.

NEW MERRITT: Cory doesn't want us to move from Los Angeles and didn't want me to even consider this job. And, apparently, when Royce called to invite me to interview, Cory took the call. *(To MERRITT)* I take it your mysterious friend Scott I never heard of before is still alive and well and there's no funeral at all? Or maybe no Scott at all?

ROYCE: *(To* MERRITT*)* So you're not Merritt at all? You're just...acting?

MERRITT: I *am* Merritt. That's Cory! Who somehow found out about this interview—

NEW MERRITT: You should have erased the phone message.

MERRITT: —And came here to ruin my chances so you can keep me in L A while you pursue your so-called acting career!

PINKY: So...who's Merritt?

MERRITT & NEW MERRITT: I am!

ROYCE: *(After a moment)* Okay, this is weird, but it's not that difficult. You're obviously not the same person. I can just call Randy Kanschat, who certainly knows what the real Merritt looks like.

CHRIS: Want me to do it? I've known Randy for years.

ROYCE: No, Chris, I can handle it.

PINKY: Can't we just cut them in half?

MERRITT: *(After everyone just stares)* Like Solomon and the baby! See, nobody gets classical references any more. Very good, Pinky.

NEW MERRITT: Royce is right—this is fairly simple. I'm Merritt and you're Cory. Let's see your driver's license.

ROYCE: Excellent. That'll prove it.

MERRITT: *(Looks briefly for wallet)* I...think I left my wallet in the hotel.

CHRIS: Convenient.

MERRITT: Or maybe it was stolen. *(To* NEW MERRITT*)* You stole it! Give me back my wallet!

NEW MERRITT: *(Taking out a wallet.)* This is *my* wallet. *(Taking out a driver's license.)* With *my* license. And *my* photograph.

(They crowd around to view the license.)

PINKY: *(To* NEW MERRITT*)* That's definitely you.

ROYCE: It is.

NEW MERRITT: And these are my credit cards, name embossed—social security, health plan, museum membership—

ROYCE: *(To* MERRITT*)* You must be out of your mind. To think you could successfully scam us.

CHRIS: Almost did.

MERRITT: I'm not scamming anybody— *(To* NEW MERRITT*)* —You are! Why are you screwing me over like this? This is my perfect job! You could act right here! It's a great theatre town!

NEW MERRITT: Please stop acting. You're getting melodramatic.

MERRITT: Cory, this is hideous! You think after this we can keep living together? How can I stay with someone who'd go to such lengths—?! *(Grabbing the license)* This is fake! The photo was inserted and relaminated! Don't fall for it!

NEW MERRITT: I think you'll find all the statistics match me, not you.

ROYCE: *(Grabbing the license, reading it)* It's true. *(To* MERRITT*)* You're a very charming person, but you have to know when to stop.

PINKY: Do you think you can figure the rest of this out in someone else's office?

ROYCE: Of course, Pinky. Chris, call everyone back and reschedule appointments for the real Merritt for after lunch. Try to explain this to everyone as succinctly as possible.

NEW MERRITT: Will what Cory's done hurt my chances? I'm really sorry about this and I'm sure people are bound to be confused, even resentful—wasting their time and all.

MERRITT: You're the one wasting their time, putting them through all this again for nothing!

PINKY: Please be quiet. You're a fraud.

MERRITT: First of all, you're wrong. Cory's very clever, but I'm the real Merritt and I'll prove it to you somehow. Second, if you interview Cory this afternoon, I can't be responsible for what happens.

ROYCE: Please, you're exposed and desperate. You'll say anything. Chris, set up those interviews.

CHRIS: Do I take them both to lunch?

ROYCE, NEW MERRITT & MERRITT: No!

PINKY: *(To* MERRITT*)* How can you threaten us? You repulse me.

MERRITT: I don't want to get hysterical. And I don't want to threaten you. But you're all being horribly— albeit it brilliantly—deceived, and there will be consequences.

(They all just stare as the lights dim, isolating MERRITT *before going out completely.)*

MERRITT: I *was* born with a caul.

END OF ACT ONE

ACT TWO

(Lights up on NEW MERRITT *and* PINKY *sitting)*

PINKY: Have you ever seen *The Fountainhead*?
With Gary Cooper and Patricia Neal?

NEW MERRITT: It's so over the top.

PINKY: The acting?

NEW MERRITT: Ayn Rand's theories.

PINKY: You don't agree with her?

NEW MERRITT: When I worked at the Howard
Johnson's national reservation center one summer,
I read all of *Atlas Shrugged* in the three-to-five second
breaks I had between customer calls. Absolutely the
best way to read that book. Although the guests—
we weren't supposed to call them customers—
often wondered why I was laughing.

PINKY: What was funny about it?

NEW MERRITT: Mostly—if you'll pardon me—the sex
scenes. Only Anne Rice writes more absurdly virile
characters. Magnificently superior specimens. So far
from reality—guess that's what people want.

PINKY: Switching gears a bit, what do you think of
Royce?

NEW MERRITT: We've only spoken briefly. You're my
first interview.

PINKY: Ah. Of course. But no...impression thus far? Of Royce?

NEW MERRITT: Not really. Should I—?

PINKY: No. Good. Wouldn't want you forming any premature opinions. Growing up, did you often ride the streetcar named Desire?

NEW MERRITT: I'm sorry...?

PINKY: In New Orleans.

NEW MERRITT: You mean the play? By what's-his-name? Arthur Miller?

PINKY: You didn't grow up in New Orleans?

NEW MERRITT: No. Oklahoma. I went to New Orleans once for Mardi Gras. Got some beads.

PINKY: Do you find Royce attractive?

NEW MERRITT: I...suppose. In a very general way. Not the kind of person I'm specifically attracted to, but attractive to some people, I'm sure.

PINKY: To what kind of people?

NEW MERRITT: I'm sorry. I think I'm missing something—

PINKY: Never mind. Do you travel to New York on museum business?

NEW MERRITT: Now and then.

PINKY: Do you know anyone at the— (*Affected accent*) Metropooooolitan Museum of Art?

NEW MERRITT: No, not really. I've been there, but, no.

PINKY: I love saying it that way—Metropoooooolitan Museum of Art. They all talk that way there, especially the outgoing director. Can you say it?

PINKY & NEW MERRITT: Metropooooolitan.

PINKY: Very good.

NEW MERRITT: I'll listen for it next time I'm there.

PINKY: Did you know their director was leaving?

NEW MERRITT: No, I hadn't heard. That's big news.

PINKY: Yes, indeed. *(Stares intently at* NEW MERRITT *for a moment.)*

NEW MERRITT: It something wrong? Food on my teeth?

PINKY: Why don't you have an Oklahoma accent?

NEW MERRITT: Oh, you know. It makes a person sound stupid. Hicky.

PINKY: Aha!

NEW MERRITT: I'm sorry. You have relatives there?
No offense.

PINKY: What's the gene pool like there in Oklahoma? Is that how everybody is? Hicky? Married to their cousins?

NEW MERRITT: It's very conservative, but not exactly Dogpatch.

PINKY: So you don't worry about the gene pool? It's our future after all—we should guard it carefully, shouldn't we?

NEW MERRITT: I don't have a strong opinion about the gene pool one way or the other.

PINKY: Oh. Good. *(Puts a hand behind back so* NEW MERRITT *can't see.)* How many fingers am I holding up?

NEW MERRITT: Um...three?

PINKY: Wrong. Four. How many now?

NEW MERRITT: Two?

PINKY: Wrong! Four again. What color am I thinking of?

NEW MERRITT: Green?

PINKY: No, red! Now?

NEW MERRITT: Red?

PINKY: No, green! Does that color mean anything to you?

NEW MERRITT: Green?

PINKY: Yes, green—dark, forest green? Does it conjure up any images in your mind?

NEW MERRITT: Trees? Grass? Algae?

PINKY: It doesn't make you want to go for a ride in a car?

NEW MERRITT: No!

PINKY: My car? My forest green Mercedes?!

NEW MERRITT: No, no, I'm sorry—I don't want to go for a ride in your car!

CHRIS: *(Appearing.)* Sorry to interrupt, but our schedule's kind of foreshortened.

NEW MERRITT: Excellent. *(Standing to go)* Is your trustee next?

CHRIS: Pinky?

PINKY: *(Distractedly)* Fine, fine.

CHRIS: *(Sotto voce to* PINKY.*)* I called Randy Kanschat to get a physical description, but haven't heard back yet.

PINKY: Good, good. Keep us on track, Chris.

NEW MERRITT: *(On the way out)* Shall we go?

CHRIS: I'll take you to Sidney if you can wait outside just a minute.

*(*NEW MERRITT *leaves.)*

CHRIS: Thanks for rearranging your schedule for us, Pinky.

PINKY: This one knows nothing.

CHRIS: You prefer the other Merritt?

PINKY: Tell Royce I much prefer *this one.*

(Lights fade out on PINKY and CHRIS. Up on NEW MERRITT waiting in a chair. After a moment SIDNEY comes in.)

NEW MERRITT: *(Jumping up, holds out hand.)* Hello, I'm Merritt.

SIDNEY: *(Holds up hand for high five.)* Sidney.

(Awkwardly, NEW MERRITT slaps SIDNEY's hand.)

NEW MERRITT: Oh, my.

SIDNEY: What? Did I do it wrong?

NEW MERRITT: You're—the One.

SIDNEY: I'm a trustee, if that's what you mean.

NEW MERRITT: I'm sorry. Never mind. I'll just have to— *(Composes self)* I'm fine. How are you?

SIDNEY: Quite well. Now before we start, I'd like to clarify that I understand about discrimination.

NEW MERRITT: *(After a moment)* Oh. Good. In the sense of circumspection and taste or—

SIDNEY: Ethnic discrimination. Prejudice. First hand experience.

NEW MERRITT: It's all around us, after all. Religious persecution, especially.

SIDNEY: I'm glad you understand.

NEW MERRITT: *(Nodding)* Underdog.

SIDNEY: Underdog?

NEW MERRITT: It's almost too painful to discuss. Incredibly anti-Semitic.

SIDNEY: What is?

NEW MERRITT: Was. *Underdog.* The cartoon in the sixties.

SIDNEY: Oh, I didn't watch—

NEW MERRITT: The villain was Simon Bar Sinister—
the evil genius. Remember what he looked like?

SIDNEY: No, I never—

NEW MERRITT: Coarse hair, thick black eyebrows,
and a big hook nose.

SIDNEY: In a cartoon?

NEW MERRITT: And he was always plotting and
inventing machines that threatened— *(Looks expectantly
at* SIDNEY*)*

SIDNEY: What?

NEW MERRITT: Polly *Purebred.* It was a recruitment
cartoon for Hitler Youth!

SIDNEY: You might be reading too much into that—

NEW MERRITT: Why do you think you never see it on
Nickelodeon?

SIDNEY: It's true I haven't seen—

NEW MERRITT: This is perfect! I'm trying to contain
myself, but—

SIDNEY: What?

NEW MERRITT: You're why I came here. Why I was
meant to come.

SIDNEY: You'll be seeing a number of people, as I
understand it.

NEW MERRITT: When you touched my hand, I felt it.

SIDNEY: *(Looking at hand)* I had a cinnamon roll, but I
washed—

NEW MERRITT: I am blessed!

SIDNEY: Um...this is a semi-government institution, so—

NEW MERRITT: *(Pulling out a vial attached to a necklace)* I wanna show you—

SIDNEY: —While religious freedom is certainly—

NEW MERRITT: *(Proffering the vial)* I got this in the Holy Land.

SIDNEY: What is it?

NEW MERRITT: The most holy relic of our Lord.

SIDNEY: I'd rather not—

NEW MERRITT: Touch it! God wants you to. You're meant to.

SIDNEY: No, I'm not that religious—

NEW MERRITT: Please!

SIDNEY: *(Fingering the vial)* All right, but I'd like to know—

NEW MERRITT: It's his foreskin.

SIDNEY: *(Dropping the vial.* NEW MERRITT *catches it.)* Whose?

NEW MERRITT: The foreskin of Christ. And now you've blessed it!

SIDNEY: I have not!

NEW MERRITT: Just by touching it! *(Dropping to knees, taking* SIDNEY's *hand)* Thank you!

SIDNEY: I'm Jewish, goddammit!

NEW MERRITT: Exactly! You're the One! All faiths can now unite! And I shall be sanctified! *(Gulps the contents of the vial)*

SIDNEY: No—don't!

NEW MERRITT: I believe in you! *(Rolls back head, begins speaking in tongues, with a death grip on* SIDNEY.*)* Thumma raaytu samaan jadidah was ardan jadia lianna elsamaa eloula wa elarda eloula madata wa elbahr la joujad fe ma.

SIDNEY: Um...excuse me. Merritt?

NEW MERRITT: *(Continues, as necessary, under dialogue as* SIDNEY *stretches toward the door)* Wa ana johanna raayton elmadina elmonkadassa urshelim el jadida nezilatan mina elsamaa min inda ellah monhayaatan kaaronsin mouzanatim lirajonliha. Wa samiiton sawtan aziman mina elsamai kailan houwaza maskinon ellahi maa elanas wa houa sayaskunu meehum wa hum yakunun lahu shaaban was ellah nafsushu yakun maahum ilahan lahum. Wa sayansahu ella hulhu damaatin min onyounihum wa elemawton la yakounon fe ma baadon wa la yakounon huznon wa la surakhon wa la wajaon fe ma baadon lianna eloumoura eleonla kad madat. Wa kal el jalison ala elarsh ha ana asnaon kulla shayin jadidan. Wa kal be onktub fainna hathihi elakwal sadikaton wa aminaton. Thumma kal le kad tanna. Ana huwa elalefon wa elyaon elbedayaton wa elneheyaton. Ana outti elatshan min yanboni maa elhayati majjanan man yaghleb yareth kulla shay-in wa akounon lahu ilahan was huma yakunu le ibnan. Wa amma elkhaifun wa ghayron elmouminin wa elrajissom wa elkatiloun wa elzunat wa elsahara wa abadatu elawthan wa jamii elkathabati fanesibahum fe elbuhaurati elmutakkaditta binaren wakibritiu ellathi huwa elmawtou eltham. Thumma faa elayya wahidunmin elsabaati elmalaikati ellathiin maahum elsakaaton eljamatelmamlonat mina elsabii eldarabati elakhirati wa takallama maiikaiilan halluma faourika elarous imraata elkharouf. Wa thahabab be billrouhi ila jabaliu azimin alin wa arani elmadinata elazimata urshalim elmukaddassat nazilatan mina elsamai min

indellahi laha majdu ellahi wa lamaaniha shibhu
akrami hajarin kahajari bashbin ballouriyin wa kana
laha souron azimon wa alilnwa kana laha ithua ashara
baban wa ala elabinaki ithna asharanaalakan wa
assmaon maktonbaton hiya assanaon assbatti bani
israiil elithany ashara. Mina elsharki thalthatu abwabiu
wa minaelshimali thalthatu abwabin wa mina eljanoubi
thalthatu abwabiu wa mina elgharbi thalthatu abwabiu.
Wa suru elmadinati kana lahuithne ashara assassan wa
alayha assmaaon roussouli elkharonfi elithuay ashara.
Wa ellathi kana uatakallamon maii kana maahu
kassabaton min thahibin likay yakissa elmadinata
wa abwabaha wasouraha. Wa elmadinaton kanat
mawdonaton wourabaatan toulaouha bikadri elardi.
Fakassa elmadinata bil kassabati massafata ithany
ashara alfa ghalmatin. Eltonlon wa elardon wa
elirtifaon montassawiyaton. Wa kassa souraha miaatan
wa arbaan wa arbaiinathira-aan thiraa inssanin.
Ayi elmalaku. Wa kana binaon sourihamin yashbin
was elmadinatu thahabon hakkiyyim wa assassatu
sourrielmadinati muzzayyanaton bikulli hajarin
karinin. Elassassonelwabu yashbon. Elthani yakuton
azraku. Elthalith akikonabyadn. Elrabii zumouroudon
thubabiyon. Elkhaminsu jazzaonakkikkii. Elsadisu
akkikon ahmaron. Elsahin zabarjadon. Elthaninon
zumurraudon silikkiion. Eltassiu yakkouton asfaron.
Elashiru akkikon abhdaru. Elhaddiyu ashana
asmanjounii. Elthani ashara jamashton. Wa elithua
ashara babau ithnata asharata lonlon-atan kullu
wahidin mina elabwabi kana min loulou-atinwahidatin
wa suku elmadinati thahabon nakiyyon kazujajin
shaffafin. Wa lam shayin huwa walhourouf haykaluha.
Wa tamshi shou-onbon elmukjlissina binouriha
wa moulonkon elardi yajionna bimajdihim wa
karamatihim ilayha. Wa abambouha lan tonjhlak
naharan li-anna laytan la yakounon hunak. Wa
yajionna bimajdiel-oumami wa karamatihim ilayha. Wa

lan yadkhulaha shay-ondanisson wa la ma yassnaou rajissan wa kathiban illa elmaktubbeena fe sifii hayati elkharonfi.

SIDNEY: *(At the door)* Hello, Chris? Thank god— I mean—I think we're having a breakdown—

CHRIS: *(Appearing)* What's going on?

SIDNEY: I don't know. Some kind of born-again ecstasy thing.

CHRIS: What started it?

SIDNEY: Apparently consumption of a two thousand year-old foreskin.

(They watch NEW MERRITT *speaking for a moment.)*

SIDNEY: I think, Chris, this is not the candidate for me. I have nothing against profound religious feeling—

CHRIS: So you're more interested in...the first Merritt?

SIDNEY: We have no choice. Can you imagine if this happened in front of a donor?

(They look at NEW MERRITT, *who has a spasm while speaking and foams a little.)*

CHRIS: Merritt? Merritt! *(Shakes* MERRITT, *freeing* SIDNEY's *hand.)* Wake up, it's the Rapture!

NEW MERRITT: What? Oh, gosh, I'm sorry.

CHRIS: *(Helping* NEW MERRITT *stand.)* We have to go see a curator now.

NEW MERRITT: All right. Thanks. *(Taking* SIDNEY's *hand, which* SIDNEY *gives only reluctantly.)* A great honor. And a great beginning.

SIDNEY: Thanks.

*(*CHRIS *and* NEW MERRITT *leave and* SIDNEY *collapses in a chair. After a moment* SIDNEY *picks up the relic vial from the*

floor and studies it. The original MERRITT *comes in and gives* SIDNEY *a black power salute that* SIDNEY *awkwardly returns with a grateful smile. Lights out on* MERRITT *and* SIDNEY *and up on* NEW MERRITT *and* CHRIS *walking.)*

CHRIS: Uh...everything all right?

NEW MERRITT: Cory's certainly cut my work out for me. Pinky was a trip.

CHRIS: And...Sidney?

NEW MERRITT: Intense.

CHRIS: So you're hanging in there?

NEW MERRITT: I'm not gonna let anybody down.

CHRIS: It's only a job. If it doesn't work out, *la vida es sueño* sha-boom, sha-boom. Oh, here's Hollis. Get ready.

(HOLLIS appears, looking tense but controlled.)

NEW MERRITT: Don't you want it?

CHRIS: What? Hi, Hollis.

NEW MERRITT: I understand you're a candidate.

CHRIS: Oh, sort of.

HOLLIS: You should be.

CHRIS: Don't think I could handle the politics.

NEW MERRITT: Too nice for the job? I doubt that. I wouldn't be surprised if you're stabbing me in the back. *(To* HOLLIS*)* Sorry. You must be Hollis.

HOLLIS: Merritt? For real this time?

NEW MERRITT: For real.

(HOLLIS looks to CHRIS for confirmation.)

CHRIS: We're pretty sure this time. I've got a meeting but I'll be back to take Merritt to Royce.

(HOLLIS *nods.* CHRIS *departs.* HOLLIS *gestures to a chair and both* HOLLIS *and* NEW MERRITT *sit.*)

NEW MERRITT: I really appreciate everybody taking time to see me after what happened.

HOLLIS: So. You write grants.

NEW MERRITT: That's right.

HOLLIS: *(Suddenly very jittery, more so than with* MERRITT*)* Liar!

NEW MERRITT: Pardon?

HOLLIS: As a grantwriter, you're inherently a liar. Right?

NEW MERRITT: How do you mean? I don't deliberately deceive anyone with my proposals.

HOLLIS: Deception is the most modern art. And deceiving fools, especially rich fools, is practically a moral duty. How difficult is it to dribble a Pollock? Drench canvases with white paint and call them Rymans for god's sake? Andres Serrano taking pictures of his jizz flying across the room, that other asshole shooting paint out his butt—I hate that shit. But look what it's done for me. And for you.

NEW MERRITT: A curator who hates art.

HOLLIS: Just modern art.

NEW MERRITT: You know what? *(Whispers)* Me, too.

HOLLIS: Then why are you here?

NEW MERRITT: Saint Wilgefortis.

HOLLIS: Who?

NEW MERRITT: You don't know her?

HOLLIS: I'm not Catholic.

NEW MERRITT: Me, either. But I love Wilgefortis. And you have an incredible Guido Reni painting of her.

HOLLIS: I don't get into the Renaissance galleries much.

NEW MERRITT: You might not recognize her even if you did.

HOLLIS: Why not?

NEW MERRITT: She's sort of in disguise. Wilgefortis was a virgin princess in the—I dunno—fifth century or something and wanted to become a nun. But her father wanted to marry her off to a neighboring prince to form an alliance. So the night before her wedding she prayed to Saint Peter for deliverance and woke up the next morning with a full beard.

HOLLIS: And the prince rejected her?

NEW MERRITT: Her father was so mad he had her crucified. She's also known as Saint Uncumber cause she's the patron saint of women who want to get rid of their husbands.

HOLLIS: The Guido Reni shows her crucified?

NEW MERRITT: Wearing a dark purple robe.

HOLLIS: I have seen that painting. It's beautiful. But I always thought it was Jesus.

NEW MERRITT: That's the cool part, art-historically speaking. I think she *is* Jesus.

HOLLIS: How do you mean?

NEW MERRITT: In a church in Lucca there's a statue that looks just like her—

HOLLIS: The Volto Santo! But that's an image of Christ.

NEW MERRITT: Exactly, but it isn't a traditional crucifixion because the Volto Santo Christ is *robed*. When the image was copied and found its way to northern Europe, no one knew what to make of it. Jesus wasn't supposed to be wearing a robe on the cross. That would be wrong. So instead—

HOLLIS: —The northern Europeans made up the legend of a bearded, female saint—!

NEW MERRITT: —Who was crucified. Out of pure rigidity, or desperation to believe. Then the legend came back to Italy and she was painted by Reni. That painting's an incredible metaphor for the relationship between human aspiration and self-deception.

HOLLIS: Are you sure you're just a grantwriter?

NEW MERRITT: It's Susan Caroselli's theory—one of your curators. But that's why I want to work here. I could stare at Wilgefortis for hours.

HOLLIS: You will if I have anything to do with it. A fundraiser with a passion for art!

CHRIS: *(Appearing.)* I'm sorry, we've got to accelerate things a bit.

HOLLIS: That's all right. I know what I need to know. *(Shaking* NEW MERRITT's *hand)* Thanks for restoring a little of my faith in my profession.

NEW MERRITT: Best compliment I've had today.

CHRIS: Get ready for a contrast. The next interview's going to be your hardest.

HOLLIS: I thought I was supposed to be the tough one.

CHRIS: Apparently Royce took more than a shine to Cory.

NEW MERRITT: What does that mean?

CHRIS: You're not jealous?

NEW MERRITT: Huh-uh. Don't try that. You don't even know me.

ROYCE: *(Appearing)* Oh, good, Merritt. I was in the neighborhood and thought you might like a cup of coffee while we talk.

NEW MERRITT: Terrific.

ROYCE: That is, if you're done, Hollis.

HOLLIS: Sure.

ROYCE: Chris, do you know why Ed Tuchman called?

CHRIS: He needed a file for the lawsuit. I already sent it to him, but you might want to call.

ROYCE: Merritt's more important right now. Shall we?

NEW MERRITT: *(To* HOLLIS*)* Thanks again. *(Disappears with* ROYCE*)*

HOLLIS: *(After a moment)* Looks like you've got a new boss. Unless Royce is an idiot.

CHRIS: That good, huh?

HOLLIS: Do you know our apocryphal Saint Wilgefortis?

CHRIS: That Reni painting in the stairwell?

HOLLIS: I was on the verge of telling Royce to get some sense and just promote you, but Merritt—this Merritt—is very smart.

CHRIS: Uh-oh.

HOLLIS: Why?

CHRIS: Pinky agrees with you, but Sidney thinks Merritt's anti-Semitic.

HOLLIS: Into saints is all.

CHRIS: Oh, it's a little more than that. If we don't hire the Merritt from this morning, Sidney's quitting the board.

HOLLIS: But the Merritt of this morning was a fake.

MERRITT: *(Appearing)* No, I'm not.

CHRIS: I asked you to wait in my office. Please!

HOLLIS: What are you doing here?

MERRITT: Saving my job. Cory's hoodwinking everyone. You, too?

HOLLIS: How'd you get past Security?

CHRIS: *(To* MERRITT.*)* Don't make me regret this any more than I already do.

MERRITT: You're sabotaging me.

HOLLIS: Hardly, if Chris got you back in the building—

MERRITT: At least let me talk to Royce again.

CHRIS: Royce is with Merritt right now.

MERRITT: You mean Cory. All the better. *(Leaves)*

CHRIS: No, Merritt! Cory! They're not in Royce's office. *(Leaves)*

(Lights out on HOLLIS *and up on* NEW MERRITT *and* ROYCE *who arrive with cups of coffee and sit at a cafe table.)*

ROYCE: I've been dying for this coffee. And to find out about Cory.

NEW MERRITT: Are you hungry?

ROYCE: *(Standing.)* Oh, you should have said. I'll get—

NEW MERRITT: No, I always keep snacks with me. *(Pulling a baggie of cheese from a pocket)* Discreetly, of course.

ROYCE: Is that cheese?

NEW MERRITT: Have some.

ROYCE: Thanks, now that you mention it, I'm starving. And I'm a cheese fiend. *(Tasting the cheese)* Mmmm. Well, let's get right to work. *(Pulls out a piece of paper)* I've an extensive list of questions—

NEW MERRITT: Excuse me, before we start—

ROYCE: Yes?

NEW MERRITT: Is this interview process standard? Who designed it?

ROYCE: I did, with a little help from Chris. Have you enjoyed it?

NEW MERRITT: Not especially.

ROYCE: Good. That's not the point. It's about survival.

NEW MERRITT: No one asked me anything about my job. Nothing about government grants, foundation grants, even fundraising in general.

ROYCE: *(Rattling the paper)* That's what this is. Shall we begin?

NEW MERRITT: Please.

ROYCE: *(Eating more cheese)* What was the absolute worst fundraising disaster you ever experienced?

NEW MERRITT: Wouldn't you rather hear about a triumph?

ROYCE: Everybody talks about those. I want to know how you handle a crisis.

NEW MERRITT: The worst?

ROYCE: That's right.

NEW MERRITT: Aside from this interview?

ROYCE: I'm terribly sorry things haven't gone as planned, but perhaps this will prove the best way to test your mettle.

NEW MERRITT: I was joking.

ROYCE: Oh. I wasn't. Now then, your biggest failure? A horrendous typo? A social faux pas with a major donor? A demanding corporate sponsor?

NEW MERRITT: I guess it would be *Inside the Israel Museum.*

ROYCE: *(Almost too eager)* What happened?

NEW MERRITT: The Jewish Community Foundation paid for a kosher reception for twelve hundred people. Unfortunately it was scheduled for a Saturday night.

ROYCE: So?

NEW MERRITT: The food had to be prepared before sundown on Friday so the caterers wouldn't violate the Sabbath. It was kept overnight in a refrigerator truck parked outside the museum. The weather was supposed to be hot, so the temperature inside the truck was kept low. Too low.

(ROYCE gasps, perhaps in pleasure.)

NEW MERRITT: When the sun went down Saturday night, we discovered that everything, all the food, was frozen solid. There was ice everywhere, and the wine had exploded, so you couldn't tell ice from shattered glass. More than a thousand people were starving and the best we could do was frozen carrot sticks and guacamole that one of the Special Events girls partially melted with her blow drier.

ROYCE: What did you do?

NEW MERRITT: We laughed. One of the trustees and I played marbles with frozen cherry tomatoes on the museum plaza.

ROYCE: We've no patience with that kind of mistake here.

NEW MERRITT: You understand it wasn't my scheduling.

ROYCE: Of course. It never is. Now, Cory—

NEW MERRITT: Merritt.

ROYCE: Pardon?

NEW MERRITT: I'm Merritt. You saw Cory this morning.

ROYCE: Of course. So sorry. Now, *Merritt*—

NEW MERRITT: Do I seem short to you?

ROYCE: Not particularly. Why?

NEW MERRITT: Studies show short people are often discounted or even disrespected in job interviews.

ROYCE: I hope I haven't—

NEW MERRITT: I had to take growth hormones as a child.

ROYCE: Well, now you seem—

NEW MERRITT: When my mother was pregnant she ate a lot of cheap cuts of meat—chicken thighs, rump roast—the body parts where cows and chickens get their growth hormone injections. Apparently the hormones were passed on to me, and I went into early puberty.

ROYCE: How early?

NEW MERRITT: Seven—

ROYCE: You went into puberty when you were seven years old?

NEW MERRITT: Seven *months*. I grew pubic hair, breasts, even started menstruating.

ROYCE: You...menstruated?

NEW MERRITT: At seven months! And since puberty is the last big growth spurt, they had to give me hormones till I was a teenager so I wouldn't be tiny all my life.

ROYCE: You grew breasts?

NEW MERRITT: At seven months! Can you believe it? By the way, how's the cheese?

ROYCE: Quite good. A number of varieties here, aren't there?

NEW MERRITT: I'm glad you like it. It's all natural. We make it ourselves.

ROYCE: Really? You and *Cory* live on a farm?

NEW MERRITT: No, an apartment.

ROYCE: So you buy whole milk from a dairy?

NEW MERRITT: No, we like to know where it's been.

ROYCE: You keep a cow in your apartment?

NEW MERRITT: *(Laughs)* No.

ROYCE: *(Munching away)* So this is what? Goat cheese?

NEW MERRITT: Goats are too big. We'd get evicted. Even in Los Angeles.

ROYCE: It isn't pecorino.

NEW MERRITT: Oh, no, sheep—same deal. Zoning laws.

ROYCE: *(Still chewing zestfully)* What kind of milk do you use?

NEW MERRITT: A number of different kinds. You noticed the variety. We used to keep a pot-bellied pig—

ROYCE: *(Stops chewing)* I'm eating pig cheese?

NEW MERRITT: Oh, no.

ROYCE: Good.

NEW MERRITT: That was the first piece you finished. Then when our golden retriever's puppies were born dead—

ROYCE: You—milked—a dog?

NEW MERRITT: It was a little tricky, but nothing compared to the cat.

ROYCE: *(Getting ready to spit out the cheese)* Please tell me I'm not eating cat cheese.

NEW MERRITT: No.

(After a moment, ROYCE *pulls out the very resistant cheese in a long, taffy-like string.)*

NEW MERRITT: That's human cheese.

*(*ROYCE *spits out the cheese and dangles it, not knowing where to put it.)*

NEW MERRITT: From breast milk. It turned out my sister's daughter would only eat those awful commercial products and we hate to waste anything. It aged slowly, but it was worth it. At least we think so. It's got an interesting consistency hasn't it?

ROYCE: *(Non-committal)* Mmm.

NEW MERRITT: We're trying to figure out if there's a commercial market, but I bet the minute we try to sell it every mother in the country will decide home-made is better. Someone could make a mint with breast milk home cheesery kits. Another angle we thought of is celebrity breast milk. Angelina Jolie cheese. Pamela Anderson cheese. I bet Madonna beats 'em to the market—she's so business-savvy.

ROYCE: *(After a moment)* I believe we're finished. Let me drop you off in Human Resources.

NEW MERRITT: *(As they start walking)* May I ask you a few informal questions on the way?

ROYCE: Of course.

NEW MERRITT: What's your relationship to the person in this position?

ROYCE: I'm their superior.

NEW MERRITT: Would I have my own office? I get gas.

ROYCE: *(*JEAN *appears.)* Ah. Here we are. *(Shaking hands with* NEW MERRITT*)* Thank you for a fascinating day. We hope to make a decision within the next two months.

NEW MERRITT: It's been...lovely.

ROYCE: Jean, please process Cory's paperwork and call a taxi. Good-bye.

(ROYCE *leaves.* NEW MERRITT *turns to look at* JEAN, *who just smiles shyly at first. After a moment,* JEAN *produces a butt doughnut, the kind used by hemorrhoid sufferers, and offers it to* NEW MERRITT *with a smile.* NEW MERRITT *just stares. Lights out on* NEW MERRITT *and* JEAN *and up on* ROYCE's *office, where* ROYCE *and the original* MERRITT *sit, talking.*)

MERRITT: I'm real.

ROYCE: Very.

MERRITT: I'm sure you could see that after this afternoon.

ROYCE: Cory was actually hostile to me, clearly tired of impersonating you. I'm sure the rest of the staff could perceive it. Sidney says Cory's straight out of *The Omen.*

(MERRITT *giggles.*)

ROYCE: This is funny?

MERRITT: You're going to figure out who I am by taking a poll.

ROYCE: The Director's the only one who counts. *(Into phone)* Is Pinky there?

CHRIS: *(Appearing)* Royce, Merritt is— *(Sees* MERRITT*)* Oh. The other Merritt is in Personnel and this one is—already here.

ROYCE: *(Into phone)* No, I'll go up there. *(Hangs up)* Chris, Pinky's with the Lannans in their gallery. I need to say hello to them and bring Pinky here. Can you entertain Merritt till I get back?

CHRIS: I guess. What about the other one?

ROYCE: Oh, have Personnel do whatever Personnel does. I'm sure everyone agrees with my selection.

CHRIS: *(Extremely uncomfortable)* Um...no.

ROYCE: They don't? Who—? *(Notices* CHRIS *indicating* MERRITT *is present)* Oh, it's all right. Merritt's a grown-up.

CHRIS: Jean and Sidney agree with you.

ROYCE: What about Pinky and Hollis?

CHRIS: They prefer the Merritt behind Door Number Two.

ROYCE: All the more reason for me to get Pinky alone. Call Personnel now and get rid of the other one. *(At the door)* Excuse me. *(Disappears)*

CHRIS: *(On the phone)* Jean, hi, it's Chris. We're in Royce's office and wonder if you can send Merritt over. On the way? Perfect. *(Hangs up.)*

PINKY: *(Arriving with* NEW MERRITT*)* Look who I found wandering the halls—

NEW MERRITT & MERRITT: Cory!

PINKY: What are you doing here?

MERRITT: Royce hired me.

NEW MERRITT: What?

PINKY: Without consulting me?

CHRIS: Oh, no. Royce went to get you—I thought—

NEW MERRITT: This is horrifying.

PINKY: Not to be rude, but—no, I take that back— I'm perfectly comfortable being rude to you. Joyful, even. How can you imagine we'd want to hire you after the things you said to me this morning?

MERRITT: I'm not imagining anything. Royce made an offer and I accepted it. A generous offer.

NEW MERRITT: How much?

MERRITT: I'm not telling you.

NEW MERRITT: We live together!

MERRITT: Maybe.

NEW MERRITT: I love you. Isn't that more important than a job?

(NEW MERRITT *kisses* MERRITT *passionately.* MERRITT *does not respond. Everyone else looks uncomfortable.* NEW MERRITT *breaks the kiss and looks hurt.*)

MERRITT: More important to *you.*

PINKY: Um...I'm sorry, but this conversation is drifting— rather, *careening*—into the personal, a realm entirely inappropriate for this venue.

CHRIS: But I think we're getting somewhere. Back to the King Solomon metaphor—

MERRITT: Everyone here is so sophisticated!

CHRIS: *(Indicating* NEW MERRITT*)* This Merritt values love more than the job. Obviously enough to confess to being Cory.

(NEW MERRITT *just stares.*)

CHRIS: Right? Cory?

NEW MERRITT: *(After a moment)* My name is Merritt. That doesn't mean I don't love you, Cory. You're just acting icy to—I dunno—show me how cold you think I am for considering this job.

MERRITT: You can stop considering. I've been hired.

NEW MERRITT: Stop saying that!

MERRITT: Neener, neener, neener.

PINKY: And it's not true. Or if it is, I can unhire you. That's it—get out—you're fired.

MERRITT: It's Royce's decision.

NEW MERRITT: Pinky can fire Royce.

PINKY: That's right!

CHRIS: I don't think we need to go that far.

PINKY: We've gone so far I don't even know where we are by now.

NEW MERRITT: Maybe we need to go farther. *(To* MERRITT*)* I heard what you said in Personnel about the dildo!

PINKY: Oh, dear.

MERRITT: Cory, shut up!

NEW MERRITT: You brought it up.

MERRITT: Pinky, you see—desperation! Do you want to hire someone like this?

NEW MERRITT: We never use dildos! Gross!

PINKY: Stop! Dildos or no. *(To* MERRITT*)* You will never be hired by this museum as long as I live. Never.

MERRITT: You'd rather hire an impostor? An actor? Someone with absolutely no fundraising experience whatsoever? *(To* NEW MERRITT*)* The only grant you can do is Cary Grant—and not very well, truth be told. *(To* PINKY*)* You'd rather have someone who knows nothing than someone who knows too much?

PINKY: We're not obligated to hire either of you!

ROYCE: *(Appearing)* Pinky, there you are! I've been all over the museum.

PINKY: Royce, have you offered the job to this—this—person?

ROYCE: Of course not. I'd never act without consulting you.

(They all turn to look at MERRITT.*)*

MERRITT: I never said it was a *formal* offer.

PINKY: *(Pushing* NEW MERRITT *forward.)* Royce, this is who you should hire.

ROYCE: Are we *actually* selecting a Grants Manager with both candidates *in the room?*

NEW MERRITT: Um...all three candidates. *(Indicates* CHRIS*)*

ROYCE: Oh, no.

NEW MERRITT: I think we need to be clear about the competition.

PINKY: *(To* CHRIS*)* You're a candidate?

ROYCE: Chris, you know I can't seriously—

CHRIS: No, of course not. I know how Development works.

MERRITT: So do I. But not everyone does. *(To* NEW MERRITT*)* What's N E A stand for?

NEW MERRITT: National Education Association.

*(*ROYCE, CHRIS *and* PINKY *gasp.)*

MERRITT: Wrong!

NEW MERRITT: When did Julian Schnabel die?

MERRITT: Exactly? I dunno. Sometime during the war.

PINKY: Which war?

MERRITT: World War Two.

NEW MERRITT: Wrong! Frida Kahlo was married to who?

MERRITT: Senor Kahlo?

PINKY: *(Raising a hand)* Diego Rivera!

MERRITT: What's the deadline for federal indemnity?

NEW MERRITT: June fifteenth.

ROYCE: Nope!

NEW MERRITT: What does Ganesh look like?

MERRITT: A river. A big dirty river—in China!

NEW MERRITT: Hardly!

MERRITT: What's a 501(c)3?

NEW MERRITT: A...new brand of Levi's?

CHRIS: *(Counting off fingers)* National Endowment for the Arts, Diego Rivera (Pinky was correct), October one and April one—twice a year (which makes that a trick question), Ganesh is an Indian god with an elephant's head—the remover of obstacles, a 501(c)3 is a nonprofit organization such as an art museum, and Julian Schnabel is—alas—still alive.

ROYCE: *(Aghast, to both MERRITTs)* You don't know anything about art or fundraising.

PINKY: Neither of you.

NEW MERRITT: You know enough to steal my identity, but not enough to steal my job!

MERRITT: I don't know you at all. And you don't know me. I've got what Royce wants.

(MERRITT kisses ROYCE as passionately as NEW MERRITT kissed MERRITT earlier.)

PINKY: Now, here—!

ROYCE: Merritt, what are you—?

NEW MERRITT: You disgusting fuck! *(Lunges at MERRITT)*

ROYCE: *(Struggling to get away from MERRITT)* Just cause I believed in you—!

PINKY: *(Lunging at* MERRITT*)* You psychic shit—!

*(*MERRITT, NEW MERRITT, ROYCE *and* PINKY *grapple during the following overlapping dialogue.)*

MERRITT: Assault! Is that how far you'll go to get a job?

ROYCE: *(Pushing* NEW MERRITT *away)* Get off me, you apocalyptic asshole!

NEW MERRITT: And you're a shitty actor! You were horrible in *The Cherry Orchard!*

*(*CHRIS *picks up the phone as if answering it, even though it hasn't rung.)*

CHRIS: Good afternoon, Development.

MERRITT: You stunk in that Peter Sellars thing!

CHRIS: Yes, just a moment.

PINKY: You're both maniacs! Security!

CHRIS: Merritt! Cory!

NEW MERRITT & MERRITT: *(Turning toward* CHRIS*)* What?

CHRIS: It's your agent.

(Both MERRITT *and* NEW MERRITT *lunge for the phone, fighting for it.)*

MERRITT: I'm expecting a callback!

NEW MERRITT: He hasn't called me in two months—!

MERRITT: *(Getting control of the phone)* Hello? Hello? Hell—

(Both MERRITT *and* NEW MERRITT *gasp—they're caught.* MERRITT *looks at* CHRIS*.)*

MERRITT: Dial tone.

NEW MERRITT: It didn't even ring.

*(*CHRIS, ROYCE *and* PINKY *stare at* MERRITT *and* NEW MERRITT, *who look extremely sheepish.)*

PINKY: Thank you, Chris. At least someone has presence of mind.

ROYCE: Pinky, should I call security?

PINKY: A wee bit late, Royce. How did this get this far?

ROYCE: I—don't—understand. Merritt had an incredible resume—

NEW MERRITT & MERRITT: I do!

PINKY: You can write anything on a piece of paper!

ROYCE: And a glowing reference from that Kanschit person—!

PINKY: If you worked for me, I'd lie just to get you to leave!

ROYCE: I'll check with Human Resources. There were a few other resumes that looked good—

PINKY: No! You're not putting us through this torture again. *(To* CHRIS*)* You're hired, promoted, whatever. *(To* ROYCE*)* No argument. Chris is the only competent person in your department.

CHRIS: But I don't *want* the job.

PINKY: Why not?

ROYCE: Pinky, this is outrageous.

PINKY: Is it salary? I can give you twice what's budgeted.

CHRIS: No, it's not—

ROYCE: Completely insulting. You're undermining me.

PINKY: Extra vacation, a museum credit card—

ROYCE: Pinky, if you force me to hire Chris—!

CHRIS: I still don't want it—

ROYCE: I'm tendering my resignation!

PINKY: Accepted!

CHRIS: I'll take it.

(They all stare.)

CHRIS: I'll take the job.

ROYCE: Pinky, you can't fire me. *(Intimately, in* PINKY's *ear)* I know too much.

PINKY: I didn't fire you. You resigned. In front of witnesses. *(To* MERRITT *and* NEW MERRITT*)* Cory, Merritt, whatever your names are, get out of here. Go back to California and never come here again, even to look at the art.

MERRITT: *(Leaving)* I hate art anyway.

NEW MERRITT: *(Leaving)* And who'd wanna work here? Everyone's insane.

PINKY: *(Stopping* CHRIS *before* CHRIS *can speak)* Thank me later. Make sure those two leave the building. Then I'll need to talk to you. I want you to take over the Development Department in an acting capacity.

*(*CHRIS *goes.)*

ROYCE: Pinky. What a lot of dramatics.

PINKY: I'll have Jean process your final check.

*(*ROYCE *just stands there, open-mouthed.)*

PINKY: How could you?

ROYCE: I—I—I was deceived, just as you were—

PINKY: I certainly was.

ROYCE: They were very clever—

PINKY: How could you let that *impostor*— *(Struggling)* —touch you?

(They stare at each other from across the room as the lights slowly dim. Lights come up on MERRITT *and* NEW MERRITT

*standing side by side under a streetlamp, looking grumpy.
They are dressed for winter. Offstage, the sound of a
champagne cork. After a moment, CHRIS appears, also
dressed for winter. They look up at CHRIS. They all freeze,
looking very serious. CHRIS pours a glass of champagne with
great ceremony. Slowly MERRITT and NEW MERRITT start
to grin. After a moment CHRIS grins, too. MERRITT and
NEW MERRITT reveal champagne glasses. CHRIS fills them.)*

CHRIS: *(Toasting)* To apocryphal saints!

(They raise their glasses and laugh uproariously.)

THE END